HAUNTING: WHITEHEAD & MIES

VICTORIA WATSON

An AIR Grid Publication

ISBN: 97809928768-7-6

INTRODUCTION

This book is about an architectural design research project based on a study of Mies van der Rohe's self-proclaimed interest in the thought of the British mathematician and philosopher, Alfred North Whitehead. The research question asks: what was *'this thing'* Mies believed he had begun to share with Whitehead in 1926? The answer is sought where Mies said he set it down, i.e., in his buildings and it is given in the discursive essay and architectural proposition set out in this book.

Haunting: Whitehead & Mies is a re-working of an earlier publication of the same title, published in 2015 by the Big Air World. It is a supplement to */Atmosphere/: The Origin of AIR Grid*, which was published in 2018 and was based on the author's original doctoral thesis of 2004.

PART ONE

The material pyramids of Egypt are a conception, what is actual are the fragmentary experiences of the races who have gazed on them.[1]

It is not true that we are directly aware of a smooth running world, which in our speculations we are to conceive as given. In my view the creation of the world is the first unconscious act of speculative thought; and the first task of a self-conscious philosophy is to explain how it has been done.[2]

Alfred North Whitehead, 'Space Time and Relativity'

The first part of this text begins with Mies van der Rohe's interview of May 1959, with the British Broadcasting Corporation, where he referred to 1926 as having been, for him, an especially auspicious year. A month later, in June 1959, in an interview for the architectural periodical Interbuild, he explained why:

In my interview with the BBC I talked of the three people in Europe who, although I didn't know them, were thinking in 1926 what I was thinking. Their business was to get this thing clear in their minds and to write their books about it. In the same way I had to build and I was very happy with the results.[3]

It is worth pausing to take in what Mies was getting at here. He was saying, just as the three people he mentions had to get *'this thing'* clear in their minds, so as to set it down in writing, he, as an architect, had to get *'this thing'* clear in his mind so as to set it down, not in writing but in building.

Turning to Mies' BBC interview. On that occasion Mies had been asked for his thoughts on the role of the architect in relation to evident changes taking place in cities. It was in the context of discussing changes to cities that Mies talked about the auspicious year and, in so doing, gave the names of the three people whom he would, later, refer to in the Interbuild article and whom he regarded as important thinkers:

I think we are just at the beginning of changing the cities, but not in a Romantic way. I am quite sure that the economical situation will have a great influence on the way our cities will be. I don't believe that we architects can just plan a city out of the blue sky. There are economical forces, they are so strong, we cannot change (them), they can be guided that is all. There is this problem of the idea in relation to the objective facts and that was quite unknown and unclear until Max Scheler, a philosopher from Cologne, wrote his book on the forms of knowledge in society. There he really clarified this problem. That was in fact a very interesting year, 1926. In this year Rudolf Schwarz wrote his book on technology, there again for the first time this problem was really clarified. And in the same year, in '26, Whitehead started his talks which he later published under the title Science and the Modern World, a strange year! [4]

According to the information given in the book's subtitle, Mies had the date wrong, it was in 1925 that Whitehead gave the talks that would form the basis of *Science and the Modern World*, but since Mies was not claiming to have actually heard Whitehead's talks, or to have read his book, that he got the date is not so important.

In the various discourses that have arisen around the cultural figure of Mies' his interest in Whitehead's thought has attracted little attention. The lack of interest might be because there is some ambiguity as to when Mies did actually begin to read Whitehead's books, or it might be because no one cares for the trouble of revising the history of twentieth century architecture, inevitable if Miesian architecture were to be understood as involved in the kinds of ontological speculations stemming from Whitehead's process philosophy.

At the time of his death, in 1969, Mies' library included Science and the Modern World in an edition of 1948,[5] but in 1926 Mies was still living in Germany and there is no reason to suppose he troubled to read English in those days. Science and the Modern World was not available in German. But it is worth noting, in the Interbuild interview Mies was not claiming to have actually read anything written by Whitehead as early as 1926. What the interview does reveal is Mies' belief in the autonomy of ideas. For what Mies was claiming in 1959, is that it was not necessary to actually read Whitehead in order to share his ideas.

In his Interbuild article, Mies made his belief in the autonomy of ideas quite clear, where he suggested a new idea can dawn in human consciousness by appearing, simultaneously, but independently, in different minds, each one preoccupied with a different domain of thought and endeavour. It seems Mies did not believe direct contact between individuated minds was strictly necessary for the dissemination of ideas. By implication, he believed influential ideas can get into the minds of individual thinkers, somehow emerging there of their own accord. He used the metaphor of the plant, or tree, to understand intellectual history, where ideas grow and ripen like fruits. As he explained in the Interbuild article, when the tree of history is ripe with an idea then *'great people who may never know each other can talk, simultaneously, about the same things.'* [6]

The question driving the research and architectural proposition that follows in this book asks: what was *'this thing'* Mies believed he shared with Whitehead? The answer is sought where Mies says he set it down, i.e., in the buildings he designed.

Science and the Modern World

In Science and the Modern World, the mathematician and philosopher, Alfred North Whitehead, made the case for a new system of concepts that he thought were necessary to re-shape the scientific understanding of nature. He used the term 'organic' to distinguish his new system from the old, 'materialistic' system it would replace. But, more importantly, Whitehead used the term organic to distinguish his new system from, what was in those days, a new idea that had spread from natural science into the general public awareness, that being the theory of relativity. Whitehead wanted to make a distinction between his system and the theory of relativity, because he thought there was a problem with relativity. Not a problem with the theory per se, but a problem with its popular reception, which seemed to encourage, as Whitehead put it, *'an extreme subjectivist interpretation':*

I mean that the relativity of space and time has been construed as though it were dependent on the choice of the observer. It is perfectly legitimate to bring in the observer, if he facilitates explanations. But it is the observer's body that we want, and not his mind. Even this body is only useful as an example of a very familiar form of apparatus.[7]

Whitehead wanted to steer the concept of relativity away from Romantic notions of subjectivity back to where it had arisen, i.e., in the objective study of matter and energy. In a scientific experiment, the human observer is conceived as part of the apparatus, they are not the subject of inquiry. Whitehead was troubled by the popular reception of relativity because it seemed to be fostering false and highly misleading notions of individual liberty. Whitehead's criticism of relativity did not mean he was against the idea of personal liberty, quite to the contrary, he was very interested in it, which is why he offered his theory of organism as the basis for *'a thorough going objectivism.'*

A crucial ingredient in Whitehead's organic theory is the elimination of cognitive activity as an essential factor in the positing of what it is to be aware. Whitehead used the notion of *'prehension'* as a means of avoiding the presuppositions that tend to come with concepts such as cognition and perception. In the following quotation, notice how carefully Whitehead state what he meants by prehension, alluding to a mode of apprehension, which *'may, or may not be cognitive':*

The word perceive is, in our common usage, shot through and through with the notion of cognitive apprehension. So is the word apprehension, even with the adjective cognitive omitted. I will use the word prehension for uncognitive apprehension: by this I mean apprehension which may or may not be cognitive.[8]

One way Whitehead developed his concept of prehension was through a careful re-reading of George Berkeley's doctrine of 'immaterialism.'

Whitehead turns to Berkeley's questioning of what is meant when statements refer to *'the reality of nature'.* He builds up an answer by quoting from Berkeley's book Alciphron. In the quoted passage, Berkeley's protagonists, Alciphron and Euphranor, are talking about a castle, both of them can see the castle, but it is some distance away from where they are standing:

Euphranor. Tell me, Alciphron, can you discern the doors, window and battlements of that same castle?
Alciphron. I cannot. At this distance it seems only a small round tower.
Euph. But I, who have been at it, know that it is no small round tower, but a large square building with battlements and turrets, which it seems you do not see.
Alc. What would you infer from thence?
Euph. I would infer that the very object which you strictly and properly perceive by sight is not that thing which is several miles distant.
Alc. Why so?
Euph. Because a little round object is one thing, and a great square object is another. Is it not so?....[9]

Berkeley's solution to the conundrum of how it is possible for the same entity to appear differently when seen from differing points of view, promoted an extreme form of idealism, sometimes referred to as 'subjective idealism.' Berkley's solution posits the ultimate reality of nature as a unity of ideas, whose medium of unification is conceived as the mind of an absolute God. Whitehead did not find Berkley's solution at all satisfactory, he formulates an alternative, where the presupposition of a supreme cognising agent is not necessary.

Whitehead argues it is not the idea of the castle, existing absolutely in the mind of God that binds the distant building to Alciphron's visual perception of it. Rather, it is a prehension **here and now**, in the place of Alciphron, of an entity **there and now**, in the place of the castle, which is sensed by Alciphron as being in some **other** place:

This unity of a prehension defines itself as a 'here' and a 'now,' and the things so gathered into the grasped unity have essential reference to other places and other times. For Berkeley's mind, I substitute a process of prehensive unification. In order to make intelligible this concept of the progressive realisation of natural occurrences, considerable expansion is required, and confrontation with its actual implications in terms of concrete experience.[10]

What if *'this thing'* Mies shared with Whitehead, was the later's concept of *'prehensive unification.'* And what if the architect understood his practice as an opportunity to expand Whitehead's thesis and to test its implications in terms of concrete experience?

On Colour

By substituting his concept of prehensive unification for Berkeley's ideas in the mind of God, Whitehead was not eliminating ideas from his organic theory of nature, but he was offering an alternative understanding of what an idea is. Whitehead preferred to use the expression *'eternal object,'* rather than idea. In what follows Whiteheads terminology is adopted.

In order to illuminate the role of eternal objects in the process of prehensive unification, Whitehead asks his reader to imagine them self as situated at some point A, where they can see some green leaves, reflected in a mirror. Try to imagine you are Whitehead's imaginary reader at A. You are looking into a mirror, reflected in the mirror is the image of some green leaves, located behind your back. He asks you to consider the greenness of the leaves and the difference of that leafy greenness as between the mirrored image and the actual leaves. Notice how his request draws your attention to the imprtance of location in what you perceive:

For you at A there will be green; but not green simply at A where you are. The green at A will be green with the mode of having location at the image of the leaf behind the mirror. Then turn round and look at the leaf. You are now perceiving the green in the same way as you did before, except now the green has the mode of being located in the actual leaf.[11]

As Whitehead acknowledges, *'there is no mystery about any of this,'* looking into a mirror and seeing the image of what is behind you is a familiar experience. But it is precisely in such a familiar, everyday structure of relationships that eternal objects can be seen to play a part in the formation of what is real. Eternal objects enter into our experience of the world about us as the modalities of phenomenal presence. In the case of the mirrored leaves, one modal presence is the colour green, another is the colour's location: **in** the leaf.

In Whitehead's organic theory it is the entangled modalities of eternal objects that actually constitute the things we human perceivers tend to refer to as *'objects of sense.'* Whitehead is uncomfortable with the notion of sense objects because he thinks it gives rise to the mistaken belief that sense objects are the basic realities of the way we experience our world. For Whitehead the basic realities of experience are not sense objects but events, which are in turn the loci of a continuous process of prehensive unification of eternal objects.

There is a second kind of object involved in Whitehead's organic theory of nature, which he terms an *'enduring object.'* To illustrate what he means Whitehead gives the example of a rock, but a building could serve just as well. An enduring object is an event that keeps on happening, in other words it is the same pattern of eternal objects recurring across a locus of events. But for all it keeps on happening, an enduring object cannot escape the passage of time, eventually it ceases to exist. Only eternal objects are exempt from the passage of time.

In the following passage Whitehead gives the example of a mountain and a colour to convey what he means on the one hand by an enduring object and on the other by an eternal object:

The mountain endures. But when after ages it has been worn away, it has gone. If a replica arises, it is yet a new mountain. A colour is eternal. It haunts time like a spirit. It comes and goes. But where it comes, it is the same colour. It neither survives nor does it live. It appears where it is wanted. The mountain has to time and space a different relation from that which colour has.[12]

A Whiteheadian eternal object is nothing outside of the events it appears in. Yet, through their shared participation in events, varieties of eternal object will qualify and mutually pattern one another. Where there is no recurrent pattern in the flux of eternal objects then, presumably, there is no endurance. If we try to imagine what such a world would be like, as seen from a human perspective, it would be a flow of continuous sensations, rather like the 'pure feeling' that Kasimir Malevich speculated about in his non-objective art.

Eternal Objects in Miesian Architecture

Mies never used expressions like 'eternal object,' and 'pure feeling,' yet there is plenty of evidence in the archives of his interest in the human experience of space. One example is related to the Farnsworth House, which was designed by Mies and built in Plano, Illinois, between 1945-'50. One story about the house tells of an article, published in the magazine House Beautiful, attacking the house on nationalistic lines, claiming it posed a threat to the American way of life.[13] Mies did not address the criticism directly, but he did respond. He stated: *'the Farnsworth House has never really been understood'* and then proceeded to talk about the house in terms of one particular type of eternal object, namely colour:

I myself have been in this house from morning to nightfall. Until then, I had never realised how colourful nature could be. Inside neutral tones have to be carefully used since all colours exist on the outside. These colours change continuously and completely, and I'd like to say that it is simply glorious.[14]

Notice how Mies presents the house as a space,

carefully seperated out from the colours of nature outside. And notice too how he describes those colours as continuous and changing. Mies' distinction between inside and outside is not unlike Whitehead's distinction between enduring and eternal objects that we looked at above in the examples of the mountain and colour. Recollect the importance of differential space and time in that distinction, where the *'mountain has to time and space a different relation from that which colour has.'* In Mies' remarks on the Farnsworth House the house is an enduring object, it frames the colours he sees on the outside. The colours do not endure, they come and go, always the same, neither surviving nor living, haunting his day at the house, from morning to nightfall.

Mies' remarks on colour are reminiscent of another important colour experience from the history of architecture. This one was recounted by a visitor to the Crystal Palace, way back in the nineteenth century. Richard Lucae, an architect from Berlin, had visited the extensive iron and glass structure. He tried to describe what it was actually like to apprehend a large volume of air, bound inside an enormous glass room,[15] in doing so he wrote:

We are in an artificially created environment that has already ceased to be a space. We are separated from nature but yet we are scarcely conscious of it; the barrier that separates us from the landscape is barely perceptible...We find ourselves so to speak in a piece of sculpted atmosphere. The sun's rays come to us not through individual openings. They fill the space with a completely beautiful naturalness. And as the sun of this space does not give or allow the light to be anything special or particular, so we must also be content with the fact that the colours borrow their limits from the objects outside. In this way it is like a magical, poetic form of light.[16]

Notice how bemused Lucae was by his experience of the enormous glass room, he refers to it as, simultaneously, a space and not a space, finally settling for the notion of *'sculpted atmosphere.'*

What is common to Mies and Lucae is the way they both attempted to describe their respective glass room in a manner that can easily be translated into Whiteheadian spatio-temporal categories. Whether consciously or not, Mies and Lucae structure their respective descriptions so as to represent the glass room as a species of enduring object, while the colours, pressing in from the outside, appear to belong to an entirely different spatio-temporal domain, Lucae even refrs to it, somewhat romantically as 'magical.' In the world of colours outside the coming and going of eternal objects is patterned more freely and does not give rise to the recurrent pattern of building that endures on the inside.

PART TWO

The second part of this text is a reading of Mies' final building, the New National Gallery in Berlin (from here on referred to as the NNG). It looks at the NNG through the lens of Whiteheadian spatio-temporal categories, concluing with a suggestion for a new kind of spatio-temporal object that might be made to appear there.

Three years after his BBC interview, in 1962, Mies was invited by the municipality of Berlin to design a new building for their city, the immediate purpose of the building was to function as a museum-gallery for the collecting and exhibiting of modern art. The records show Mies began work on the NNG in 1962, construction was completed in 1968, just one year before his death in 1969.

The NNG is characterised by the dominant feature of a large, single-roomed enclosure placed on top of a podium. The room is constituted by three elements, a paved-floor, which is synonymous with the top surface of the podium, a roof-plate and a glass-screen. The roof-plate, a square figure in plan, is supported on its perimeter by eight slender, tapering columns, cruciform figures in plan, two on each side. With the supporting columns pushed to the perimeter, the large room below consists in a broad expanse that is almost, but not quite, empty. The glass-screen, hanging down from the roof-plate on all four sides, is set back from the edge by an equal dimension all the way around. The roof-plate over-sails the room under it to create an outdoor covered space, the effect of which is to circumscribe the large room in an ambulatory (figure 1).

Inside the large room there are only four interruptions to the air/space, two mechanical ducts rise as large shafts of Tinos marble to the underside of the roof-plate, and two clusters of low-level screens rise to just above head height. The screens differentiate a specific portion of space for cloakroom storage and are located next to the two stair openings, holes in the floor-slab, which lead down into the basement. The basement houses a number of gallery spaces, administrative offices and library, a coffee shop, toilets, rooms for mechanical plant and various storage spaces. To the back of the basement the floor-slab is cut away and there is a garden (figure 2).

For a person who visits the NNG, regardless of their direction of approach, it is not the large room that appears first, what appears first is the roof-plate, a large steel grid, painted black that looks as if it is floating, hovering, silently, above the surface of the podium. It is beautiful, stark, startling and obvious. In Whiteheadian terms the grid is an eternal object, captured here in the enduring form of the black, steel roof-plate, which it dominates. (figure 3).

Figure 1

Doctor Watson Architects (DWA), electronic model, Mies van der Rohe (MvdR), design of the New National Gallery in Berlin (NNG), frontal view with partial transparency

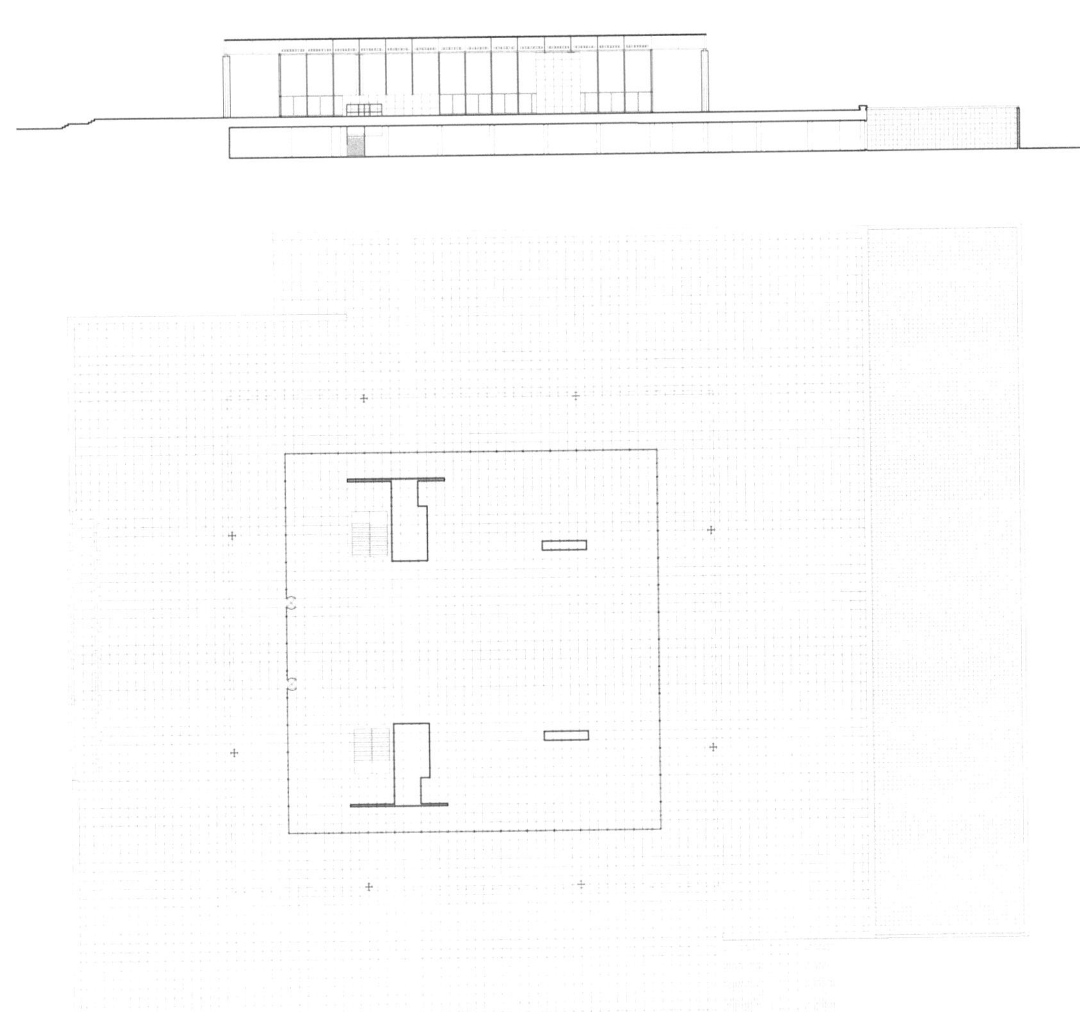

Figure 2

DWA, electronic model, MvdR, NNG, plan at podium level and East-West section, showing the location of the garden at the back

Figure 3

DWA, electronic model, MvdR, NNG, External View, looking from the North-eastern limit of the podium towards the temporary exhibition hall

By studying published drawings of the NNG it is possible to ascertain key dimensions of the roof/grid. It is: 1.8 metres deep, ordered on a 3.6 x 3.6 metre module, eighteen modules from front-to-back and eighteen modules from side-to-side. The eight columns supporting it are 8.1 metres high, which means the proportional relationship between the depth of the grid and the air/space underneath it is 2:9.

The columns reach down from the roof/grid to the paved-floor of the podium. Between the paved surface of the podium and the top of the roof/grid there is an implied modular striation of space, the unit of measure being ninety centimetres. The air/space between the paved surface of the podium and the top of the roof/grid is striated eleven times, nine times between the podium and the underside of the roof/grid and twice between the underside and the top of the roof/grid; between the ninth and tenth striations is a narrow zone of separation, acknowledging the pinned connection holding the roof/grid to the tops of the supporting columns (figure 4).

The system of spatial striations is an eternal object, captured within the enduring object that is the building, in three ways. First in the glass-screen hanging down from the underside of the roof-grid. The glass-screen consists of glazed panels, set within a black framework of slender steel. There is one horizontal division of the frame, it marks the third of the nine striations dividing the air/space between the paved-floor of the podium and the underside of the roof/grid. Second, in the low-level screens that delineate the areas for cloakroom activities. These screens rise to the same height as the framing division of the glass-screen, in other words, they too mark the third of the nine striations dividing the air/space between the top surface of the podium and the underside of the roof/grid. Third, in the two identical rectangular shafts, symmetrically placed and clad in panels of green Tinos marble. The shafts function as service ducts, presumably they contain pipes, conduits and mechanical equipment. The shafts appear to reach-up to the underside of the roof/grid, although it is not clear if they touch it. The marble panels are cut to correspond to the spatial rhythm of the eight striations drawn through the air/space between the paved surface of the podium and the underside of the roof/grid, dividing it into nine equal parts (figure 5).

The eternal objectivity of the system of spatial striations is tentatively made to appear in the enduring objects that sculpt the air/space between the paved surface of the podium and the underside of the roof/grid.

Turning now to the space below the podium, or rather inside it. The podium serves as an enormous basement for the NNG and, as we have seen, houses a variety of functions essential to its operations as a public museum.

Figure 4

DWA, electronic model, MvdR, NNG, External View, looking along the North-eastern wing of the ambulatory, showing the twinned columns forming part of the roof-support armature

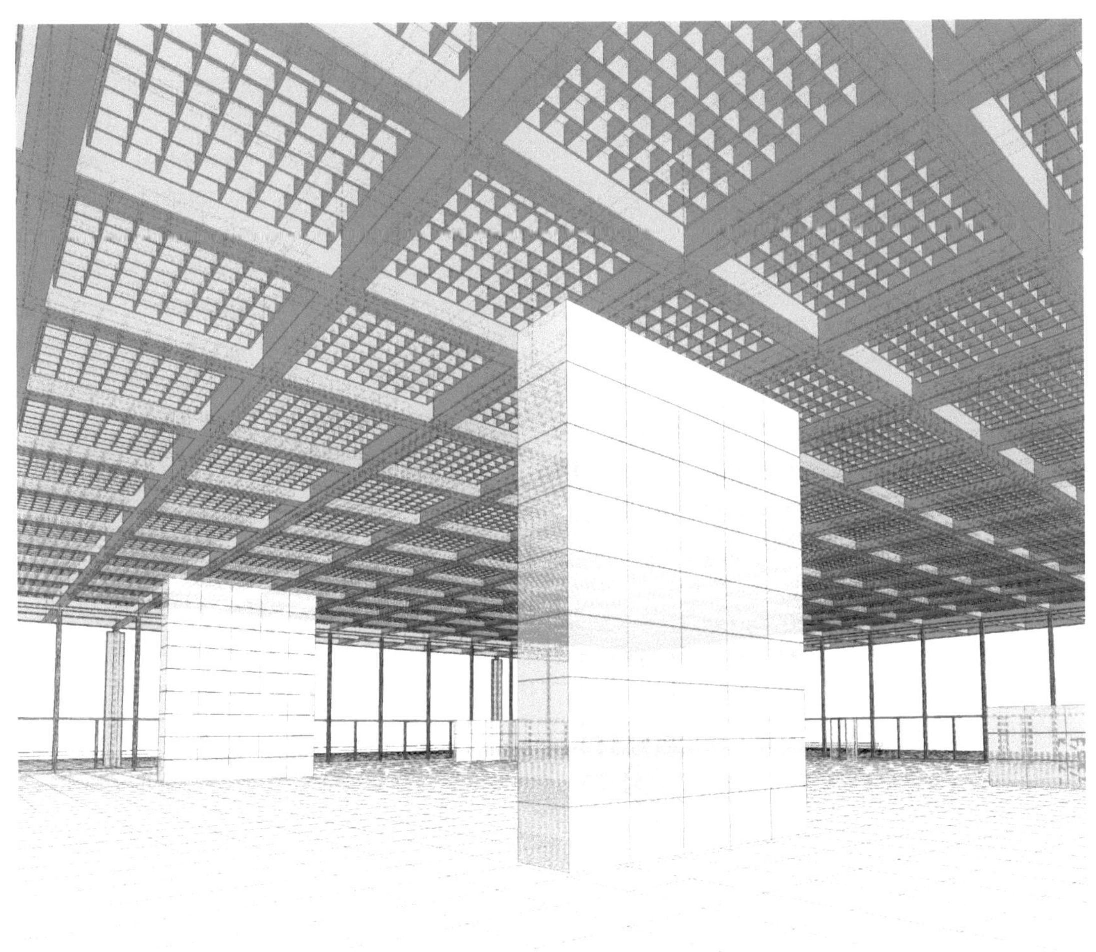

Figure 5

DWA, electronic model, MvdR, NNG, Internal View, looking obliquely across the temporary exhibition space, from the South-western corner, towards the shafts of Tinos marble

Between the basement floor and the basement ceiling there are no physical marks and therefore no clues as to the presence, or not, of an eternal object ordering the basement air/space. Furthermore, the distance between the topside, paved surface of the podium and the underside, tiled ceiling, is unknown!

In fact there is an eternal object ordering the basement air/space, it can be found by turning to the garden at the back (figure 6). The walls enclosing the garden are lined with slabs of stone, which are coursed in what appear to be even bands. From the underside of the parapet that stands up on the top surface of the podium, to the basement floor, there are eight striations and one narrow band of separation. The separation band sits between the bottom of the parapet and the first of the eight striations dropping down to the basement floor. The band plus two of the eight striations corresponds to the depth of the podium and the remaining six correspond to the airspace between the basement ceiling and the basement floor (figure 7).

The actual dimension of the striations drawn into the basement air/space is more difficult to ascertain than the ninety centimetre divisions drawn into the air/space of the large room above. However, the ratio between the respective volumes of air is in the proportion of thirteen below to eighteen above.[17]

The analysis given so far establishes eternal objects, in the mode of horizontal planes, striating the sculpted atmosphere of the NNG; but what about the other direction, is there an equivalent system of vertical planes? If so, what is the relationship between these and the horizontal planes and how, as the NNG endures, do they appear together? One way to answer these questions is by attending to the paved surface of the podium. The podium is a rectangular figure, very nearly square, its surface is marked by the coursing of stone paving slabs that capture the eternal object of a 1.2 metre square grid.

Between the podium paving/grid and the ground of the surrounding city space there is a change in level, i.e., the paving/grid is raised up in relation to the ground datum of the city, which means the limits of the paving/grid are clearly delineated. In fact, the change in level between the raised up figure of the paving/grid and the ground datum of the city falls away from front to back, with the main steps up to the podium located on the side closest to the datum of the city. The change in level means the visitor's journey across the paving/grid is accompanied by an increasing feeling of detachment from the datum of the city (figure 8).

The feeling of detachment is characterised by two dominant perceptions. On the one hand, an increased awareness of the ambient light in the air, on the other,

Figure 6

DWA, electronic model, MvdR, NNG, External View, as if sitting on the garden wall, looking back over the garden towards the podium and temporary exhibition space

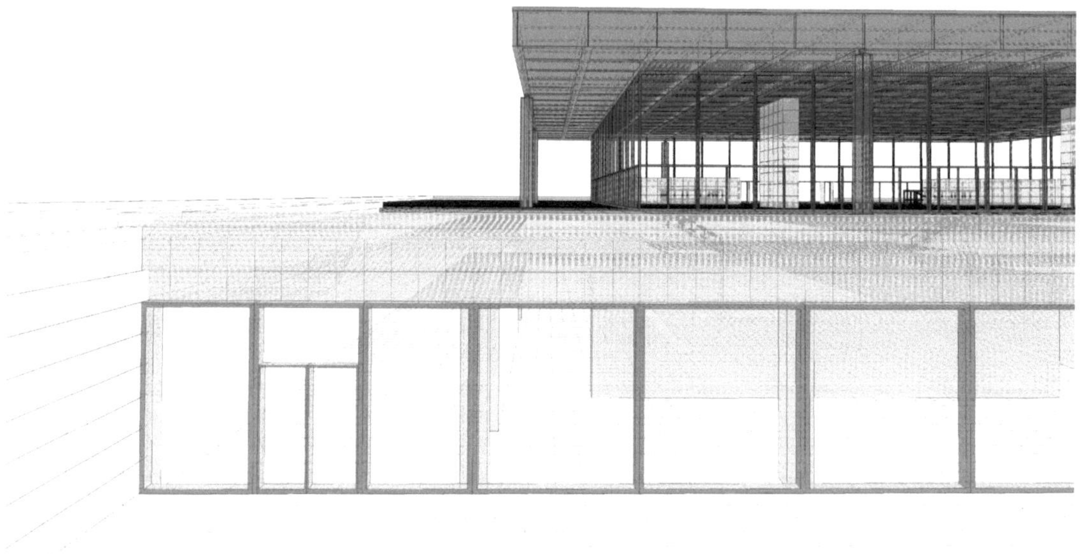

Figure 7

DWA, electronic model, MvdR, NNG, External View, showing the coursing of the garden wall and the flow of the paving grid into the hollow-podium-basement

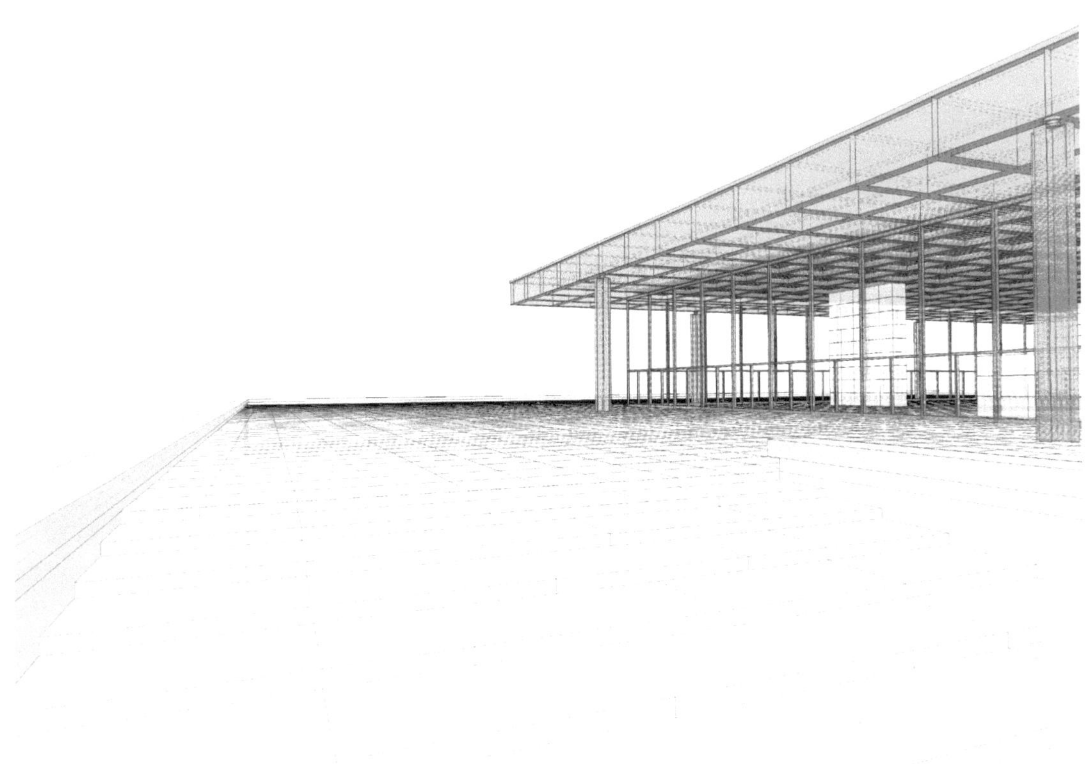

Figure 8
DWA, electronic model, MvdR, NNG, External View, showing the steps leading up and onto the podium from the South-eastern corner of the site

an increased awareness of the grid pattern that appears in the paving layout. As the paving/grid approaches the glass-screen hanging down from the roof/grid, the screen's slender mullions appear in the field of perception. The mullions seem to continue the pattern of the paving grid, as if it turns upwards, through ninety degrees to rise in perfect alignment with the roof/grid above. The mullions of the glass-screen are but one example of the way a system of vertical planes can be seen to intersect with the system of horizontal planes, the pair fusing together to striate the air/space of the NNG into a single eternal object. The glass-screen draws together the paving/grid and the roof/grid, binding them into a closed relationship. In facilitating the drawing together of the paving and roof grids it is out of the question that the vertical members of the glass-screen are literally supporting the roof/grid, they are too fine and slender to even support their own weight, let alone that of the big black roof/grid floating over them. Their presence reads as necessary for the appearance of the eternal object, but not for the practical function of holding the roof/grid up in the air (figure 9).

As well as turning and drawing upwards as it meets the glass-screen, the paving/grid continues on its horizontal trajectory, flowing under the screen and into the air/space inside.

Within the air/space of the large room the flow of the paving/grid is challenged on three occasions. First, where it meets the low-level screens of the cloakroom areas, here it rises to turn through ninety degrees, as if up and over the screens. Second, where it meets the vertical shafts of Tinos marble, again the grid rises to turn through ninety degrees, up and over the shafts. Third, where it meets the holes in the floor-slab leading down into the basement, here the grid disappears (figure 10).

The grid appears again on the underside of the floor-slab, i.e., on the basement ceiling, but now it is captured in the organisation of the ceiling tiles. The modular dimension of the ceiling/grid does not coincide with that of the paving/grid above, but there is a clear and unequivocal relationship between them, the two grids are simply off-set, with the module of the ceiling/grid precisely half that of the paving/grid above. From the ceiling/grid, columns drop down to the basement floor and there, on the floor, the eternal object of the paving/grid reappears, as if mirrored across a virtual plane, located half-way between the top-side of the podium and the basement floor. The vectors of the grid are carefully aligned on the centre-face of the columns dropping down from the ceiling/grid. The shift of the ceiling/grid, in relation to that of the floor, is another example of the way in which the patterns of spatial vectors striating the NNG air/space are fused together into a single eternal object (figure 11)

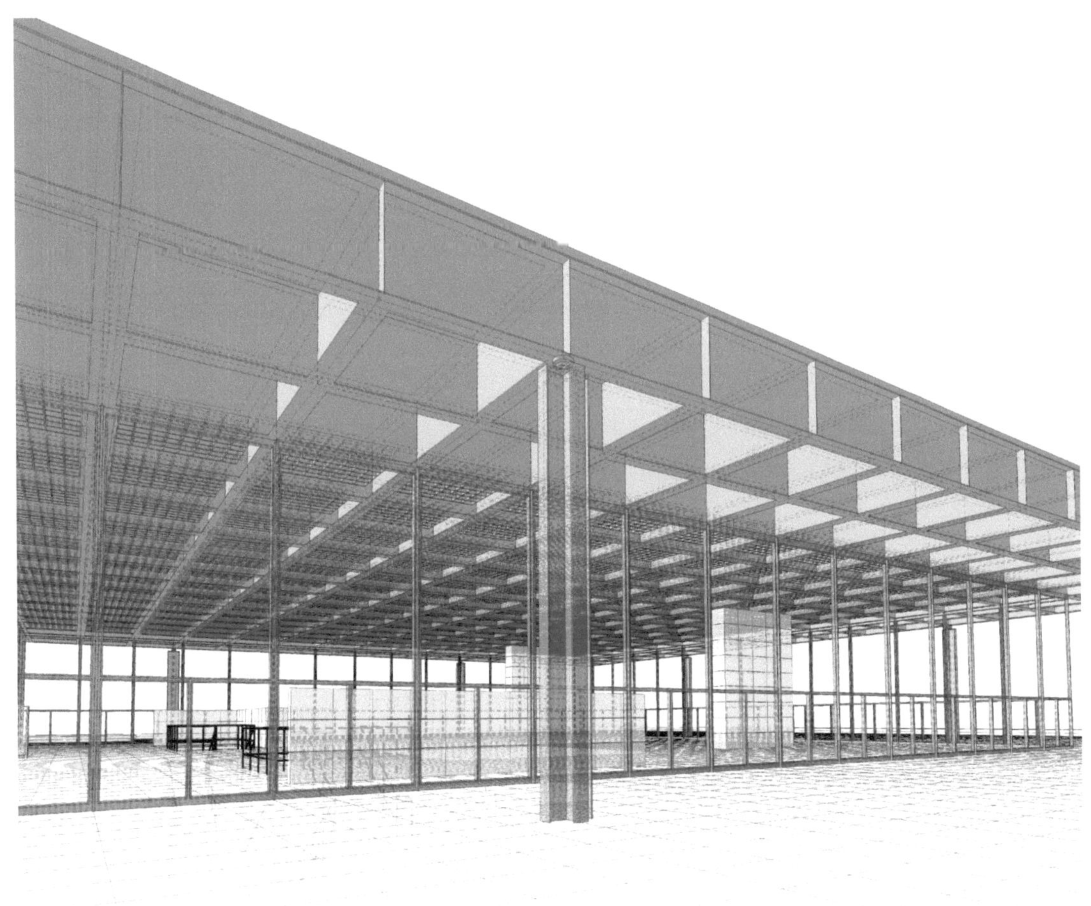

Figure 9

DWA, electronic model, MvdR, NNG, External View, showing the detail of the column to roof junction and the recessed glass 'curtain wall' that hangs down from the roof and encloses the temporary exhibition space

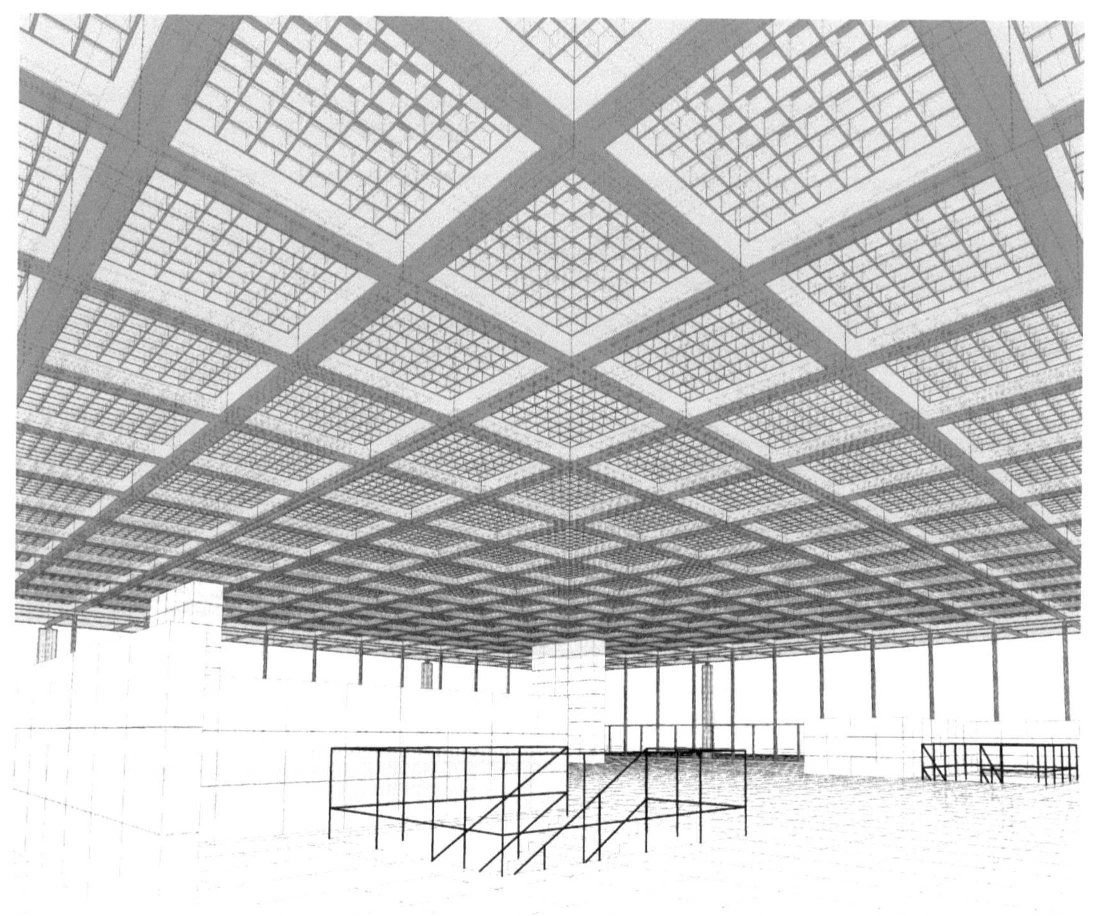

Figure 10

DWA, electronic model, MvdR, NNG, Internal View, looking obliquely across the temporary exhibition space, from South-East to North-West

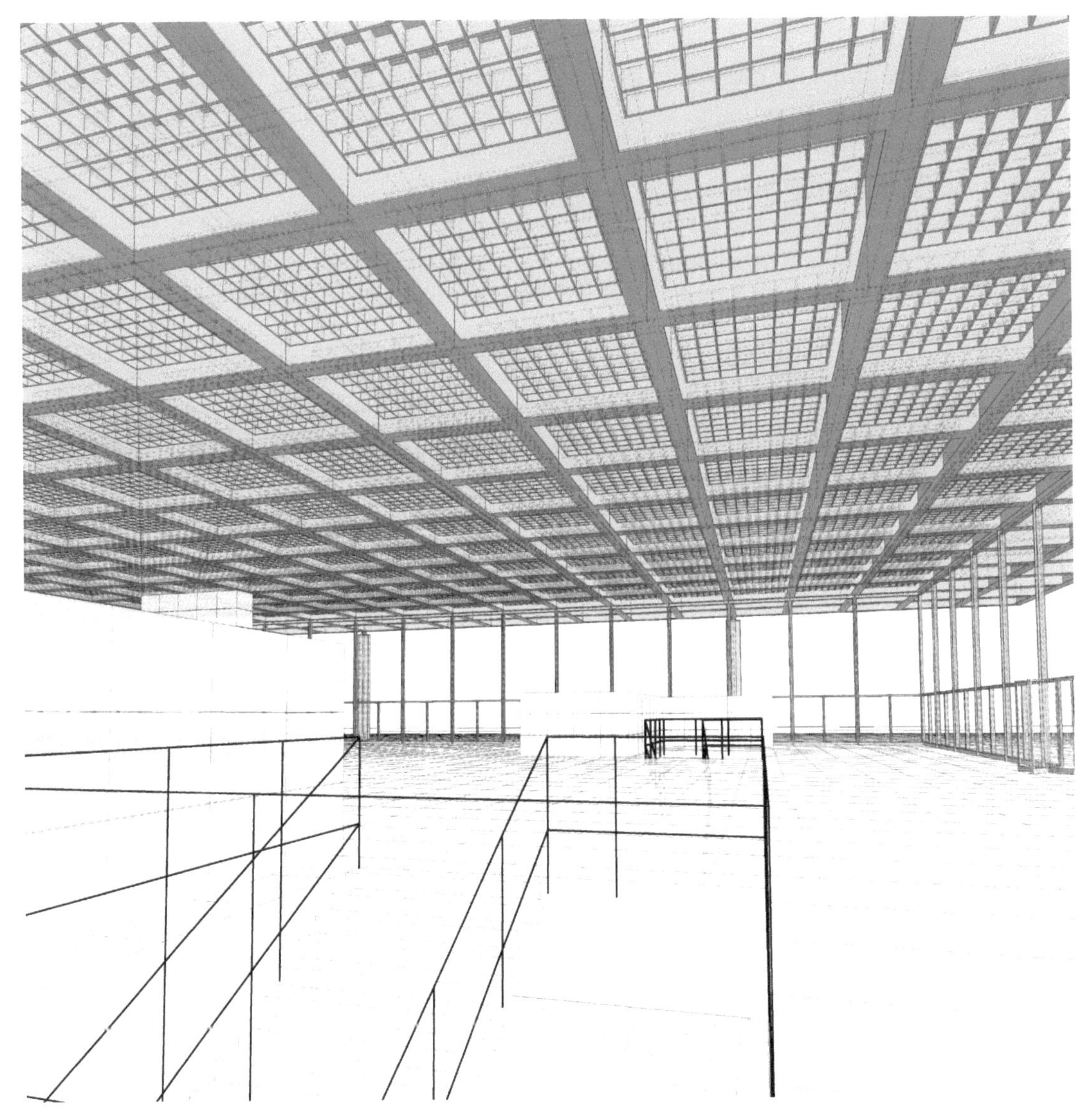

Figure 11

DWA, electronic model, MvdR, NNG, Internal View, looking across the stairwell and cloakroom zone of the temporary exhibition space

Proposition

Once the single eternal object, recurrent in the endurance of the NNG air/space, has been identified, then it becomes available as a mental device for imagining new species of eternal object. There are many possibilities, but the one selected for this study begins by reassembling the NNG eternal object in the form of an electronic model, one that will be built inside a computer. As our analysis shows, NNG air/space consists of a number of elementary building components that are fused together into a single, enduring object by the eternal object that patterns and binds them together in structured and measured relationships. The proposed electronic model is interested in these patterning and binding relationships, however, it is not interested in representing the enduring objects in which they appear and disappear. The proposed electronic model replicates the patterning and binding relationships only, which are constructed inside the computer as a series of lattice forms, each one expressed as a colour. There are four such lattices, their colours are: white, grey, ultramarine and pale blue.

One thing architects often do with electronic models is attempt to create illusions of sense objects, such as the textures of timber, concrete and glass and the effects of light and shade. But where one is modelling the patterning and binding relationships only, these having been abstracted from the enduring objectivity of the actual building, then the question of rendering sense objects does not arise, for there are no sense objects implicated in the model, put simply, there is nothing to render.

Another thing architects often do with electronic models is to inhabit them with the representation of human figures. Sometimes these are placed in the model to convey a sense of scale, sometimes to communicate ideas about the way the proposed spaces will be occupied and used. Since it is the eternal object only that we propose to represent in our electronic model we are led to the question of who, or what, are the logical inhabitants of such a model? According to the Whiteheadian manner of thinking adopted in this research, the answer to the question is given in the concept of *prehensive entity.*

As we saw at the start of this essay, a Whiteheadian prehension is an *'apprehension that might or might not be cognitive.'* The 'might' or 'might not ' is important here, because Whitehead wanted human thought and feeling to be understood as just one possibility arising in nature, but not as nature's supreme acheivement. For Whitehead, the creation of a smooth running world is the outcome of a continuous process of prehensive unification, it is a process that does not necessarily produce human experience. However, where human experience is produced, then the kinds of prehensions involved may be characterised by an awareness of eternal objects.

One of the best known places to find events haunted by objects of the eternal kind is in the Homeric epics, where the gods and goddesses appear and disappear from the scenes of human life. In Homer, when the gods and goddesses are not haunting some place on Earth, they are usually on Mount Olympus, where they live in the house of the leading deity, Zeus.

The family of haunting characters, invented to inhabit our electronic model of the eternal objectivity of the NNG is based on the Homeric gods and goddesses, there are 14 of them. Each divinity is constructed as a lattice form and composed of a unique selection of colours. The Eternals are made to haunt the patterning and binding model of the eternal objectivity of the NNG.

In the fourteen picture plates that are reproduced in the concluding pages of this book, the staged appearances and disappearances of the Eternals are captured and captioned as objects of sense for human viewing. In looking at them please do not mistake them for events, i.e., for moments of the continuous process of prehensive unification, but please try to see them for what they actually are: colour drawings, made inside a computer and printed with ink on paper. At the same time, do bear in mind, the fact that you can see them at all is thanks to the continuous process of prehensive unification, by way of which there is an actual world.

PLATE 1, Zeus, lord of the bright lightening and of the dark cloud

The son of Cronos spoke, and bowed his dark brow in assent, and the ambrosial locks shook on the king's immortal head; and he made great Olympus quake.[19]

PLATE 2, Leto, the honoured consort of Zeus

Leto gathered up the curved bow and the arrows that had fallen here and there among the whirl of dust. She then went back, taking her daughters bow and arrows.[20]

PLATE 3, Apollo, who strikes from afar

Down from the peaks of Olympus he strode, angry at heart, with his bow and quiver on his shoulders. The arrows rattled...and his coming was like the night.[21]

PLATE 4, Hera, of the golden throne

With this she anointed her lovely body and she combed her hair, and with her hands plaited the bright tresses, fair and ambrosial, that streamed from her immortal head.[22]

PLATE 5 Athene, daughter of the mighty sire

Then she stepped on to the fiery chariot and grasped her spear, heavy and huge and strong, with which she vanquishes the ranks of men, those with whom she is angry.[23]

PLATE 6, Poseidon, the shaker of earth

And in three ways have all things been divided, and to each has been appointed his own domain. I indeed, when the lots were shaken, won the grey sea to be my home.[24]

PLATE 7, Hephaestus, famous god of the two lame legs

The bellows, twenty in all, blew on the melting vats, sending out a ready blast of every force, now to further him as he labored hard, and again in whatever way he wished.[25]

PLATE 8, Hermes, beyond all in the cunning of his mind

He bound beneath his feet his beautiful sandals, immortal, golden, which bore him over the waters of the sea and over the boundless land swift as the blasts of the wind.[26]

PLATE 9, Ares, the bane of mortals

You have the unbearable, overpowering spirit of your mother; her can even I scarce control by my words. So it is by her promptings, I imagine, that you suffer these things.[27]

PLATE 10, Iris, the messenger of the immortal gods
Up, go, swift Iris; leave the seat of Olympus and announce in Ilios to great-hearted Priam that he go to the ships of the Achaeans to ransom his dear son.[28]

PLATE 11, Aphrodite, the laughter loving daughter of Zeus

She spoke, and loosed from her bosom the embroidered strap, inlaid, in which are fashioned all manner of allurements; in it is love, in it desire, dalliance and persuasion.[29]

PLATE 12, Artemis, huntress of the golden arrows

A mighty hunter he was, for Artemis herself had taught him to shoot all wild things that the mountain forest nurtures.[30]

PLATE 13, Dione, the fair goddess

She clasped her daughter in her arms, and stroked her with her hand and spoke to her, saying: Now who of the sons of heaven, dear child, has done such things to you? [31]

PLATE 14, Dionysus, the joy of mortals

Dionysus fled and plunged beneath the wave of the sea, and Thetis received him in her bosom, filled with fear, for mighty terror got hold of him at the man's shouts.[32]

Notes

1. Alfred North Whitehead, 'Space, Time and Relativity,' *The Aims of Education and other essays*, The Free Press, 1929, 162
2. Ibid, 163-164
3. Mies van der Rohe, 'No Dogma,' *Interbuild Vol 6, No 6, June 1959,* 11
4. http://web.archive.org/web/20060304201901/http://www.bbc.co.uk/bbcfour/audiointerviews/realmedia/vanderrohem/vanderrohem5.ram
5. See, Werner Blaser, 'Some books from Mies' library,' *Mies van der Rohe, Continuing The Chicago School of Architecture*, Birkhäuser Verlag, Basel, Boston, Stuttgart, 1981, 299-303, 302
6. Mies, 'No Dogma,' *Interbuild, 1959*, 10
7. Alfred North Whitehead, *Science and the Modern World, Lowell Lectures, 1925*, The Free Press, 1925, 118
8. Ibid, 69
9. Ibid, 68
10. Ibid
11. Ibid, 71
12. Ibid, 86-87
13. See the account in, Franz Schulze, *Mies van der Rohe, A Critical Biography*, The University of Chicago Press, 1985, 252-259
14. Mies van der Rohe, quoted in, Werner Blaser, *Mies van der Rohe, Farnsworth House*, Birkhäuser, Publishers for Architecture, Basel, Boston, Berlin, 1999, 23
15. In the canonic histories of modern architecture it is sometimes noted that Miesian architecture owes something to the iron and glass palaces of the 19th century, usually it is the tectonic idea of the framed enclosure that is used to make the connection. For an outline of the influence of 19th century iron and glass structures on developments in 20th century architecture see, Kenneth Frampton, *Studies in Tectonic Culture*, The MIT Press, Cambridge, Massachusetts, London, England, 1995. For an account that is specific to Mies see, Peter Carter, 'Structural and Spatial Concepts,' *Mies van der Rohe at Work*, Phaidon Press, London, 1999, 15-35
16. Richard Lucae, 'On the Meaning and Power of Space in Architecture,' Harry Francis Mallgrave (ed.), *Architectural Theory Volume I, An Anthology from Vitruvius to 1870*, Blackwell Publishing Ltd., Oxford, 2006, 558 - 560. The Crystal Place was erected in Hyde Park for the Great Exhibition of Art and Industry of 1951 and subsequently removed and resurrected at Sydenham, Lucae's account refers to the Sydenham site.
17. DAW is indebted to Matthew Butcher for helping to ascertain this ratio
19. Iliad, 1.527-530
20. Iliad, 21.502-504
21. Iliad, 1.44-47
22. Iliad, 14.175-177

23 Iliad, 5.743-745

24 Iliad, 15.190-193

25 Iliad, 18.470-472

26 Iliad, 24.340-343

27 Iliad, 5.891-893

28 Iliad, 24.141-144

29 Iliad, 14.214-216

30 Iliad, 5.51-53

31 Iliad, 5.371-374

32 Iliad, 6.134-137

Bibliography

Werner Blaser, *Mies van der Rohe, Farnsworth House*, Birkhäuser, Publishers for Architecture, Basel, Boston, Berlin, 1991

Werner Blaser, *Mies van der Rohe, Continuing The Chicago School of Architecture*, Birkhäuser Verlag, Basel, Boston, Stuttgart, 1981

Peter Carter, *Mies van der Rohe at Work*, Phaidon Press, London, 1999

Kenneth Frampton, *Studies in Tectonic Culture*, The MIT Press, Cambridge, Massachusetts, London, England, 1995

Ludwig Hilberseimer, *Mies van der Rohe*, Paul Theobold, Chicago, 1956

Harry Francis Mallgrave (ed.), *Architectural Theory Volume I, An Anthology from Vitruvius to 1870*, Blackwell Publishing Ltd., Oxford, 2006

Moisés Puentes (ed.), *Conversations with Mies van der Rohe*, Princeton Architectural Press, New York, 2008

Franz Schulze, *Mies van der Rohe, A Critical Biography*, The University of Chicago Press, 1985

Gabriela Wachter (ed.), & Peter Craven (trans.), *Mies van der Rohe's New National Gallery in Berlin*, Vice Versa Verlag, Berlin, 1995

Victoria Watson, /Atmosphere/: The Origins of Air Grid, AIR Grid, 2018

Alfred North Whitehead, *The Aims of Education and other essays*, The Free Press, 1929

Alfred North Whitehead, *Science and the Modern World, Lowell Lectures, 1925*, The Free Press, 1925

Paul Kahlfeldt, Gerwin Zohlen (eds.), *Neue Nationalgalerie Berlin, Dreissig Jahre*, Paul Kahlfeldt, 1998

www.ingramcontent.com/pod-product-compliance
Ingram Content Group UK Ltd.
Pitfield, Milton Keynes, MK11 3LW, UK
UKHW060101300726
14090UKWH00003B/333

* 9 7 8 0 9 9 2 8 7 6 8 7 6 *